Rasa Rhythms Of Soul

A Collection of Soulful Poems

Sejal Kimta

BookLeaf Publishing

India | USA | UK

Made with ❤ on the BookLeaf Publishing Platform
www.bookleafpub.in
www.bookleafpub.com

Dedication

To my revered local deities, Raromool Khadasan, Shirgul Maharaj and Maa Deuinder, whose boundless blessings have been my constant source of strength and guidance, lighting my path and empowering my journey forward.

Preface

Rasa The Rhythms of Soul presents 21 poems, each meticulously crafted with a delicate poetic style. The poems delve into the timeless themes of women's empowerment, divine grace and the often overlooked lessons of life. In the rush of modern existence, these essential truths are too often neglected or forgotten. Yet, within these pages, each poem serves as an invitation to pause, reflect and reconnect with the deeper currents of our being. The verses spark an inner curiosity, prompting the reader to reconsider their own path and purpose. Far more than mere words, these poems offer a profound call to awaken the soul and rediscover the wisdom that shapes our lives.

Acknowledgements

I am deeply grateful to all those whose unwavering support, encouragement, and love have made the creation of this book possible.

First and foremost, I wish to express my heartfelt gratitude to my parents, Mrs. Anita Kimta and Mr. Rajneesh Kimta, whose boundless love and guidance have been the foundation of my strength. To my grandparents, Mrs. Shakuntla Kimta and Mr. Roshan Kimta, whose wisdom and values continue to inspire me. To my aunt and uncle, Dr. Poonam Kimta Chauhan and Dr. Ankur Chauhan whose constant encouragement to pursue my passion for writing and to make a meaningful impact in the world has been a guiding light.

To my younger sisters, Bhavya Kimta and Aaradhya Chauhan , your constant affection has been a source of joy and encouragement. To my best friend, Divya Rathore, your patience and companionship have been invaluable throughout this journey.

A special note of thanks goes to my maternal uncle and aunt, Mr. Amit Azad and Mrs. Pooja Azad, whose steadfast belief in me has always been a source of motivation.

Finally, I am indebted to all my family members, whose collective love, support and belief in my vision have played a paramount role in shaping this book. Without their presence in my life, this work would not have been possible.

Thank you, each and every one of you, for being the pillars that have supported me throughout this journey.

1. Shri Krishna

Krishna,
My lotus-eyed
Dusky creator, your
Charm baffles me. "Wait till you see my Radha,"
Said Kanha.

2. God's Trial

Upon a defeat in the bloodied field the princess
screamed, "Why me? O Lord!"
"The fiercest battles are for the strongest souls," replied
the Almighty God.

3. She Who Endures

She, who stands when all seems wrong,
A quiet strength that moves along.
She, who stumbles, feels the fall,
But rises up and gathers all.
She, who's seen as home's embrace,
Yet shapes the world with quiet grace.
She, who gives without a sound,
And walks through life, both lost and found.

4. Visage

I gazed at the mirror,
Sighed in grief.
Held my tears back,
And again, glowered at the mirror.
Black brown bruises.
Droopy dead dermis.
Bloody red eyes.

I Dropped to my knees,
Howled with sealed lips,
The visage in the mirror,
Had its soul deceased.

5. The Pounding Fear

"Oh ! How hot you look,"
Said a man with a lurk.
Quickly, I stepped back,
All ready to smack.
But the fear took me, like a fish on a hook.

6. Screams

Those cries are real,
Eyes once bright, are now sealed
With sorrow, wrapped in fear,
Where laughter lived, no cheer.

Why are they seen through bitter eyes?
Why are their pleas met with cold disguise?
What sin have they wrought?
Is it the hue they wear, or the dreams they've sought?

Isn't humanity a boundless thing?
More than the shade of skin we bring.
Is it not the heart that beats inside,
That makes us whole, that makes us guide.

The answer whispers a soft yes,
For kindness has no earthly dress.
The need is simple, the truth is clear,
A ceaseless love, to hold us all near.

7. A Vision

While basking in the sun,
I heard a faint hum.
"La la la la , my life is so fun."

A dusky vision appeared,
Where my younger self cheered.
With eyes as bright as the sun,
Chasing the vibrant butterflies, who were on a run.

"I want to be one", I whispered in flight.
In that moment everything felt just right.

With a tear gliding down my seam,
I realised it was a pretty dream,
I rose from my doze,
As a blue butterfly bedded on my nose.

8. Thy Eyes

With eyes like those,
That shine like stars,
How worthless the galaxy is,
With everything it has,
Yet not eyes like thy.

For every glare we share,
My heart skips a flare.
I try and try,
Not to be shy,
Nevertheless, thy eyes are
Warriors piercing like spar.

9. The True You

Let the world behold the true you,
It will light another's view.
Hiding feelings, veiled in night,
Cannot heal nor set things right.
Express, don't bury deep inside,
For silence turns the soul to hide.
Repress, and guilt will softly creep,
As broken moments cannot keep.

10. The Journey

The unmade journey,
Finding everything around,
Yet, empty within.

11. In Love

One in love
Is like a fish in water;
Both are incomplete
Without the other.
For the former fades,
The latter wanes away.

12. Rosy Death

The blood red and the saint white,
With the straight stem and
The lush green pointy leaves,
Entangled with thorns.

The ruffling petals, one on top of another.
Smooth and velvety like a mousse.
Fragrant and romantic,
Yet, lying on one's tomb.

13. The Tomb of Hope

Your sight of death is

My sight of hope.

Your sight of grief is

My sight of joy.

Your loss is

My liberation.

When I lay in peace,

Your cry disturbs my calm.

My love, learn the life and its lessons. No one lives for

eternal seasons.

14. The Same Horizon

The infinite stretches of blue and gold,
The tiny molecules and the granules—
To my eyes, you look the same.

The desert is a mighty ocean, and
the ocean is a colossal desert.
To my eyes, you look the same.

The curvy dunes and the wavy waves,
The forlorn camel and the lost seahorse—
To my eyes, you look the same.

Lost in either entails loss of staves;
One is fatal, and the other is grave.
To my eyes, you look the same.

15. Fate

Falling softly, one by one,
Along with the roaring wind.
The dead tree stood silent, as the
Eternal life comes to an end.

16. The Witch's Curse

Her long, black, luscious hair turned dull,
Like trees in a barren grove.
With dreaming eyes, she peeped out
And witnessed the joy young boys wove.

"O God! I wish to live like them.
Will the old witch allow it?"
The tiny girl sighed in grief.
"But maybe, that's not where you fit."

Echoed the dim old witch's voice.
With terror-stricken eyes,
The little girl howled for freedom,
As night began to rise.

17. The Oak

Under the shade of the towering oak,
I sat and heard a loud laughter.
Children's voices like pearls, softly spoke.
Their joy was pure, an untouched chapter.

Nimbly, I seized my camera's frame,
To hold their gleeful moments, free of care.
For life once was a simple joyful game,
When all we sought were chocolates and time to spare.

But now, the world is chasing after dreams,
Rushing toward an end that none can see.
A fleeting race, consumed by endless schemes,
"I think you've lost the truth," a girl said to me.

In pink she stood
And said, " All will be good. Here, have some food."

18. Fragrant Friendship

A friendship like a garden of rose,
Filling hearts with a fragrant belief.
With each passing day, the bond grows,
A friendship like a garden of rose.
The petals unfold and trust freely flows,
Curing all grief with sweet relief.
A friendship like a garden of rose,
Filling hearts with a fragrant belief.

19. The Hell

Everything was vague around,
The chilled air heard a gasping sound.
The panic within was again found.

I rose up, blood all over me.
Smirked, then looked up to see
With dreaded Tarsier eyes,

Tears of guilt began to fall, as
The psycho within roared,
"You know well, everyone within bears a hell."

20. Kindness

Keep the spirits soaring bright,
Against the dark, relentless night.
With every tear that dares to fall,
We rise, unbroken, through it all.
Lift the world with gentle hands,
Simple steps on shifting sands.
In kindness' glow, we'll find our way,
And turn the night into the day.

21. Wreaked Friendship

The creative bond we shared,
The sunny moments we cared,
The foolish bits we paired—
All came to a conclusion,
Driven by confusion,
Breaking the affinity,
And creating toxicity,
Leading to the end of a bond
That might have endured so long.

Building regret in each heart,
That we might have not been apart,
That we might have not been apart!